THE 100 MOST
MOST
BEAUTIFUL
CHINESE CHARACTERS

www.royalcollins.com

THE 100 MOST

MOST

BEAUTIFUL
CHINESE CHARACTERS

XU HUI

TRANSLATED BY JULIE LOO

 Chemical Industry Press

 ROYAL COLLINS
— *Books Beyond Boundaries* —

THE 100 MOST BEAUTIFUL CHINESE CHARACTERS

Xu Hui
Translated by Julie Loo

First published in 2022 by Royal Collins Publishing Group Inc.
Groupe Publication Royal Collins Inc.
BKM Royalcollins Publishers Private Limited

Headquarters: 550-555 boul. René-Lévesque O Montréal (Québec) H2Z1B1 Canada
India office: 805 Hemkunt House, 8th Floor, Rajendra Place, New Delhi 110008

Original Edition © Chemical Industry Press

ISBN: 978-1-4878-0771-9

To find out more about our publications, please visit www.royalcollins.com.

As well as its obvious visual appeal, China's millennia-old writing system is a carrier of the nation's culture and identity. In this book, Xu Hui selects and explains the 100 most beautiful Chinese characters with the help of eye-catching illustrations that bring their meanings alive, and historic tracings through seal script all the way back to ancient oracle bone carvings. For novices and experts alike, this translation by Julie Loo offers English readers a compelling insight into the world of written Chinese.

女 female, woman [nǚ]

| Oracle-bone 甲骨文 (c. 1400 BC) | Bronze script 金文 (c. 1000 BC) | Small seal script 小篆 (c. 200 BC) |

– The oracle bone script for this character was the image of a kneeling woman with her arms crossed.

– *Unmarried women* are referred to as 女, and *married women* are called 妇 [fù].

– According to the *Book of Rites*, when a baby boy was born, a wooden bow would be hung on the left side of the door. If the baby was a girl, a scarf would be hung on the right side.

– Because boys and girls have different physiques, 女 was extended to denote *delicate*.

车 vehicle [chē]

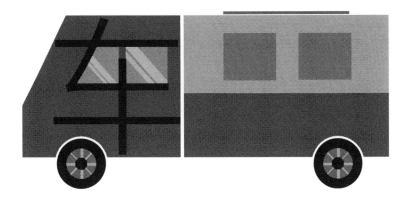

 Oracle-bone

 Bronze script

 Small seal script

 Regular script
(C. AD 25)

- The oracle bone script for this character was an image resembling a carriage with two wheels.
- *A carriage* was known as 舆 [yú]. It could carry people, or function as a storage compartment. From this idea, the character was extended to mean *numerous*, as in the phrase 舆论 [yú lùn] *public opinion*.
- In ancient times, the left seat in a carriage was viewed an honored seat. Therefore, the proverb 虚左以待 [xū zuǒ yǐ dài] *reserving the honored seat, or post* was used when the left seat was left empty for an important guest. The honored guest sat on the left, the coach driver in the middle, and the person accompanying the guest on the right. The seating arrangement was different in a chariot. The commander-in-chief sat in the middle, the coach driver on the left, and on the right was a 车右 [chē yòu] *the armed escort posted on the right in an escorted carriage.*
- The phrases 辅车相依 [fǔ chē xiāng yī] *as dependent on each other as the cheek and the jaw* and 唇亡齿寒 [chún wáng chǐhán] *mutual dependence - if the lips are gone, the teeth will be exposed to the cold* both denote interdependence.

犬 dog, hound [quǎn]

Oracle-bone   Bronze script   Small seal script

- This character refers to a large dog. A dog that does not have long, spiky hair is called a 狗 [gǒu] *dog*.
- In the Zhou Dynasty, there was an office for a 犬人 [quǎn rén] *the person responsible for dog sacrifices. Dog sacrifices* were called 羹献 [gēng xiàn].
- Sacrificial dogs were fed on people's leftover food. Fattened dogs could then be offered as 羹献 [gēng xiàn].
- Among the six domesticated animals, the horse and the dog were the fastest in speed. The phrase 犬马 [quǎn mǎ] *a dog or a horse of good breeding* emerged from this fact. Horseback game hunting was a popular sport among rulers in ancient times. Hounds were used to assist in driving the hunted animals. The phrase 声色犬马 [shēng sè quǎn mǎ] *sensual pleasures (literally – becoming addicted to songs, women, hunting, and racing)* resulted from this practice.

天 sky, heaven [tiān]

Oracle-bone   Bronze script   Small seal script

- The oracle bone script for this character was an image of a person standing erect. The most prominent part was his emphasized head.
- The idea of the character referred to a person's head. This idea was emphasized in phrases like 天灵盖 [tiān líng gài] *crown of the head*, and 天庭 [tiān tíng] *middle of the forehead*.
- The *Mandate of Heaven* had its origins in the Zhou Dynasty. Everything in the world had a predestined fate. Anything that was beyond one's understanding and control was considered 天意 [tiān yì] *the will of heaven*. A belief in divine beings in heaven developed from this concept.
- The phrase 九天 [jiǔ tiān] *the Ninth Heaven, the highest of heavens* did not refer to 九重天 [jiǔ chóng tiān] *the nine layers of heaven*. Yang Xiong in the Western Han Dynasty labelled each one of the nine layers in 太玄 [tài xuán] *Canon of Supreme Mystery, the nine layers of heaven*.

井 well, orderly [jǐng]

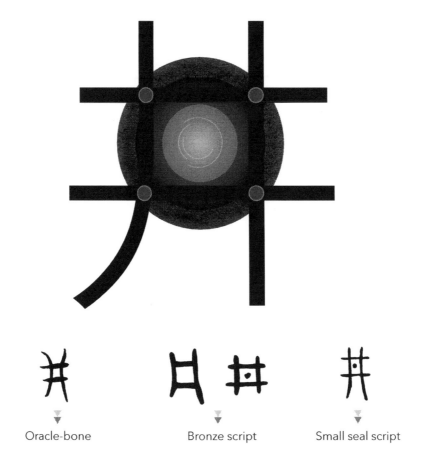

Oracle-bone   Bronze script   Small seal script

- This character has not undergone any changes over the centuries. It is still the image of a well.
- 井田制 [jǐng tián zhì] was *a land allocation system* established in the Eastern Zhou Dynasty. A large piece of land, with an area of nine hundred *mu* as a unit, was divided into nine smaller areas, resembling the character 井. Eight families shared one well. The character 井 in phrases like 井井有条 [jǐng jǐng yǒu tiáo] *in an orderly manner*, 井然有序 [jǐng rán yǒu xù] *orderly*, 背井离乡 [bèi jǐng lí xiāng] *be compelled to leave one's hometown* do not refer to the well but to 井 in the land allocation system.
- The origins of 市井 [shì jǐng] *town, market place* is highly controversial. Whatever the saying, the phrase could only be used to refer to a place within a city.
- The land allocation system worked so well that the character's meaning was extended to denote orderliness in the context of the law.

见 to see, to look [jiàn]

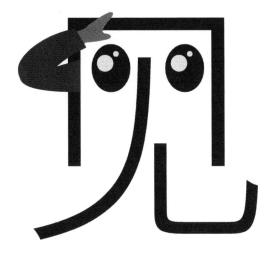

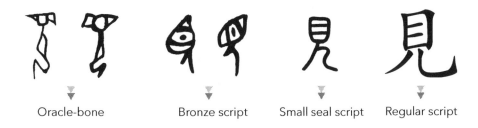

| Oracle-bone | Bronze script | Small seal script | Regular script |

- The idea of 见 is *to see, to look*. It was extended to mean 觐见 [jìn jiàn] *to present oneself before a monarch*.
- The character can also be used in reverse, to turn the action into the passive form and apply it to the self.
- As for the origin of the phrase 寻短见 [xún duǎn jiàn] *to commit suicide,* the curtain used for covering the coffin was called 见. The curtain for a person who died before adulthood was shorter than normal, and was known as 短见 [duǎn jiàn] *literally – short curtain.* Metaphorically, a person searching for a short curtain for his coffin was looking to shorten his life.

凤 phoenix [fèng]

Oracle-bone

Small seal script

鳳

Regular script

- In ancient times, 凤 referred to the male phoenix and 凰 [huáng] referred to the female.
- The phoenix had morals, righteousness, etiquette, benevolence, and faith on it as decorative ornaments, and it was a symbol of hope. *"When seen, peace will fill the world."*
- The original idea of the complex character 風 [fēng] *wind* was more than merely air moving around. It denoted the form of a mythical bird or dragon.

父 father [fù]

Oracle-bone   Bronze script   Small seal script

- The oracle bone script for this character was a compound ideograph. On the right was a hand, and on the left was a stick. The hand was holding the stick, as if the figure were teaching his children about obedience.
- *Friends of the father* are called 父执 [fú zhí].
- In ancient times, there were many requirements pertaining to the methods of avenging one's blood relations.
- 父 is also a respectful term to address an older man.

北 north [běi]

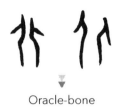

Oracle-bone

Bronze script

Small seal script

– The original idea of 北 was 背 [bèi] *to carry somebody on one's back or shoulders.* The oracle bone, bronze, or small seal script for the character was the image of two people facing back-to-back.

– Since the back signified darkness and gloom, most houses in ancient times were built facing south, to get more light. The character 北 was extended to refer to *a dark and gloomy location.*

– 北面 [běi miàn] can be used to refer to *the relationship between a teacher and a student.*

– 北方 [běi fang] *the north* denotes winter – the last of the four seasons. "In winter, everything bends its head." This back-to-back image in a bent form resembles the oracle bone version of 北. Therefore 北方 was also known as 伏方 [fú fang] *in its bending form.*

兄 elder brother [xiōng]

Oracle-bone

Bronze script

Small seal script

- This character was the base form for 祝 [zhù] *the person leading the sacrificial offering during worship*. This role was usually performed by 兄 the *eldest son*.
- In ancient times, the relationship between brothers was given great importance. Brotherly love was regarded as 友 [yǒu] *friendship*, one of the six kind deeds mentioned in the *Rites of Zhou*.
- 司马牛之叹 [sī mǎ niú zhī tàn] *the sigh of Sima Niu* refers to *being helpless and all alone, without any brothers*.

鸟 bird [niǎo]

   鳥

Oracle-bone　　　Bronze script　　Small seal script　Regular script

- This is a typical pictographic character. The oracle bone script was a vivid image of a bird with its claws clinging tightly to the ground.
- 鸟 is the general name for fowl with long tails. "隹" [zhuī] is the general name for fowl with short tails. The two names were sometimes mixed up.
- People in ancient times had a way of telling male and female birds apart. A bird with its right wing overlapping its left wing was male, while a bird with its left wing overlapping its right was female.

乐 music [yuè]

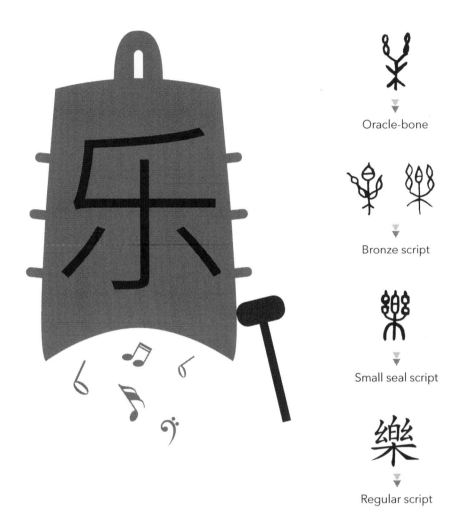

Oracle-bone

Bronze script

Small seal script

Regular script

- This is a pictographic character. There is no consensus on the name of the instrument it denotes.
- It was said that official in charge of music during the reign of the Yellow Emperor was Ling Lun. He was the pioneer of music-making.
- People in ancient times attached moral value to music. The six 乐德 [lè dé] *values in music education* were noted in the *Rites of Zhou*.
- When used to mean *something that one likes*, the character is pronounced [yào].

外 external, outside [wài]

Bronze script

Small seal script

- Divination in the ancient world was done in the daytime. If it was done at night, it indicted that there was trouble at the frontier. The ideograph 外 meant *distance*. 于事外矣 [yú shì wài yǐ] denoted that *there was trouble at the frontier*.
- 外 and 内 [nèi] *internal, within* were both words used in oracle bone divination. They were also used as divination dates in the oracle language.
- The terms 内子 [nèi zǐ] *wife* and 外子 [wài zǐ] *husband* originated from a literary couple's conversation in a poem written during the Kingdom of Liang.

册 book, volume [cè]

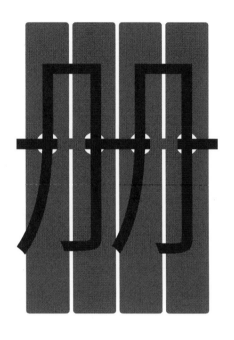

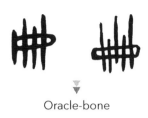

Oracle-bone

Bronze script

Small seal script

- The original idea of this character was *letters, correspondence*.
- 册书 [cè shū] was *the imperial decree from the emperor regarding the appointment of a crown prince, the conferring of honors and ranks, and other such matters*. There were eleven types altogether.
- 册祝 [cè zhù] was the earliest type of 册, used in spiritual worship, or as a prayer to the divine beings.

发 to send out, to give out [fā] / hair [fà]

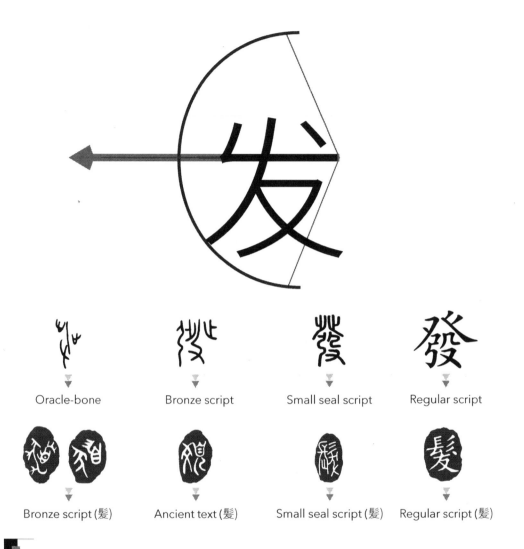

Oracle-bone	Bronze script	Small seal script	Regular script

Bronze script (髮)	Ancient text (髮)	Small seal script (髮)	Regular script (髮)

- This is one of the Chinese characters with the most meanings. Both the complex characters 發 [fā] meaning *to send out, give out* and 髮 [fà] meaning *hair* have been simplified to 发, spoken with different tones.
- All of the extensions from 发 [fā] (first tone) started with the idea of throwing sticks or shooting arrows.
- 髮 originally referred to the long hair on a dog's neck.
- *A pair of newlyweds* was called 结发夫妻 [jié fà fū qī]. The idea stemmed from braiding together a lock of hair from the husband and wife, to symbolize one heart in love.

圣 sacred, holy, imperial [shèng]

Oracle-bone

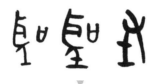

Bronze script

Small seal script

Regular script

- In ancient China, people with great wisdom and moral values who had reached human perfection were bestowed with the title of 圣人 [shèng rén] *a saint*.
- The character's symbol in oracle bone script was a person standing with his face to the right. His large ears faced left, and a mouth was added to the left. The image indicated the ability to listen and to reason.
- The phrase 圣人 was another name for *good wine*. It referred to *clear, mellow wine*, while 贤 人 [xián rén] referred to *unfiltered wine*.

成 to accomplish, to become [chéng]

| Oracle-bone | Bronze script | Small seal script |

- This is a compound ideographic character. The fact that the character's symbol in oracle bone script was a dagger has never been disputed. On its left was a short vertical line indicating the source of divergence.
- This vertical line carried the idea of a nail. A wedge or a nail was used to hold the blade of a dagger in its long handle. Once this was done, the weapon would be ready for an expedition. *Shuowen Jiezi Dictionary* explains that "成 is accomplishment, completion."
- During the Zhou Dynasty, there was an office for a judge who was responsible for implementing eight types of rules, including the governance of prisons.

达 without obstruction, to extend, to attain [dá]

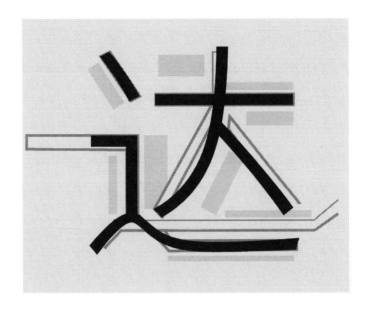

| Oracle-bone | Bronze script | Small seal script | Regular script |

- *Shuowen Jiezi Dictionary* explains this character as *walking but never meeting*, reflecting the idea of vastness. If a person could walk in the street without meeting another person, it indicated that the street was wide and clear of obstructions, allowing for a clear passage.
- 达 is the idea of *being smooth and without obstruction*. It can be extended to refer to many things, including streets, the understanding of logic or reasoning, recommendations, and popular and influential people.
- During ancient times, very detailed street divisions were made. The *Erya* (an early dictionary/encyclopedia) contains extensive references to street names; 达 was used as a unit to indicate unobstructed thoroughfares.

执 to hold, to manage, to control [zhí]

Oracle-bone

Bronze script

Small seal script

Regular script

- This is a compound ideographic character. The character's symbol in oracle bone script was a person with cuffs on his hands.
- The original idea of 执 was *to arrest, to capture*. It was extended to mean *to hold, to manage, to take charge of, to carry out*, and *to control*. The image of hands held together with cuffs to prevent escape led to the extension of the meaning to *being stubborn*.
- 执牛耳 [zhí niú ěr] *to be the acknowledged leader* originated from ritual sacrificial activities. It used to refer to the person leading the oath-taking ceremony. Now, it refers to people who are in leadership positions.

同 similar, the same as, convergence [tóng]

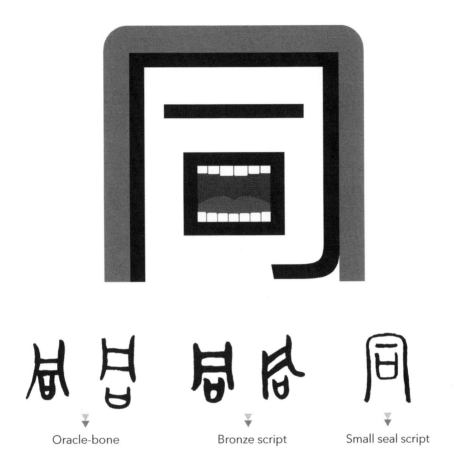

Oracle-bone   Bronze script   Small seal script

- The oracle bone script for this character was the image of a cover plate with a 口 [kǒu] *mouth* below it. This image denoted convergence or assembly.
- 同 was also used to mean 爵 [jué] *an ancient wine vessel with three legs and a loop handle.*
- Every twelve years, the dukes, princes, and high officials had a group audience with the emperor. During this ceremony, the wine cups that were used were called 同 to symbolize 会同 [huì tóng] *a joint affair.* From then on, 会同 was used as a general term for an audience with the emperor.
- 同 also referred to a defined area of land. When thunder strikes, the sound can be heard a hundred 里 [lǐ] *a Chinese unit of length about five hundred meters* away. One hundred 里 was the same as one 同, therefore the term 雷同 [léi tóng] *duplicate, identical* arose.

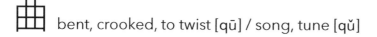 bent, crooked, to twist [qū] / song, tune [qǔ]

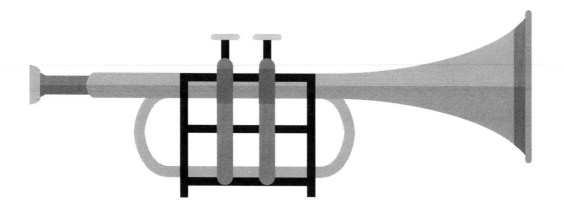

Oracle-bone   Bronze script   Small seal script

- The original idea behind this character was the apparatus for sericulture, or storage of items. To weave the containers, materials had to be bent and twisted. This led to the meaning of the character being *crooked, not straight*.
- It can also be extended to mean *a melody*. Duan Yucai, a Chinese philologist of the Qing Dynasty, stated that irregular musical tones made up a composition.
- The *chimney* was known as 曲突 [qū tū] in ancient times. The origin of this name came from an Eastern Han Dynasty scholar, Huan Tan, in one of the stories in the book *Xinlun*.

尘 dust, dirt [chén]

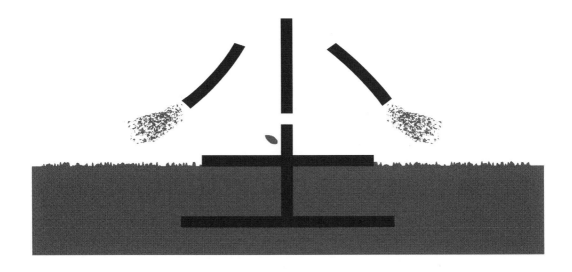

Large seal script 籀文 (c. 700 BC)   Small seal script   Regular script

— This character originally referred to the dust stirred up from the ground by a herd of deer as they galloped. The character's symbol in both the great seal and the small seal scripts was the image of a deer.

— The modern proverb 甚囂尘上 [shèn xiāo chén shàng] *to cause a great clamor* has a negative connotation. It is used to mean *rumors in the air*. However, it originally referred to the Battle of Yanling during the Spring and Autumn Period.

农 famer, farming [nóng]

Oracle-bone	Bronze script	Small seal script	Regular script

- *"Farming, the basis of world survival, is of utmost importance."* Starting in the Qin Dynasty, China established a series of agricultural advocacy offices. The job of officials in these posts was to encourage farmers to harvest mulberry and plough the land from generation to generation.
- The oracle bone script for the character 农 was the image of a farming tool. The ideograph denoted the use of tools to cultivate land in forests.
- The *Rites of Zhou* divided farmers into three categories. *Farmers living in the mountains* were called 山农 [shān nóng], *those living in the marsh* were called 泽农 [zé nóng], and *those living on flat ground* were called 平地农 [píng dì nóng].
- Farming depends heavily on the weather, and thus on the sky. People in ancient times named a star 农星 [nóng xīng] *Farmer's Star*, short for 农丈人星 [nóng zhàng ren xīng] (literally *Star of a Father-in-Law who is a Farmer*).

会 to balance an account [kuài] / meeting, association [huì]

Oracle-bone   Bronze script   Small seal script   Regular script

— This character's original meaning in the oracle bone and metal scripts was *lid of a container*.

— During the Zhou Dynasty, government officials would gather accounting staff for a monthly and an annual balancing of the country's revenue. *Monthly account balancing* was known as 要 [yào], while *yearly account balancing* was known as 会 [kuài]. This exercise was called 大计 [dà jì] *national annual accounting. Gathering the accounting staff to carry out the national accounting* was known as 会计 [kuài jì].

— 会 has another meaning. Its original idea was a lid. When a lid is placed on a container, it leaves a gap. From this idea, the extended meaning of the character is *a crevice*.

舌　tongue [shé]

Oracle-bone　　　Bronze script　　　Small seal script

- At the bottom of the character's oracle bone script was a mouth. Above the mouth was a long, forked tongue.
- *The Book of Songs* states, "A woman who has a long tongue is trouble." This is the origin of the term 长舌妇 [cháng shé fù] *a woman who gossips*.
- In ancient times, a person with a very pink tongue was regarded as a man of wisdom; a person who could touch his nose with his tongue had the potential to hold a high government position.
- As well as the ability to talk and to differentiate tastes, the tongue of Dong Ai of the Han Dynasty also had a memory.

血 blood [xiě / xuè]

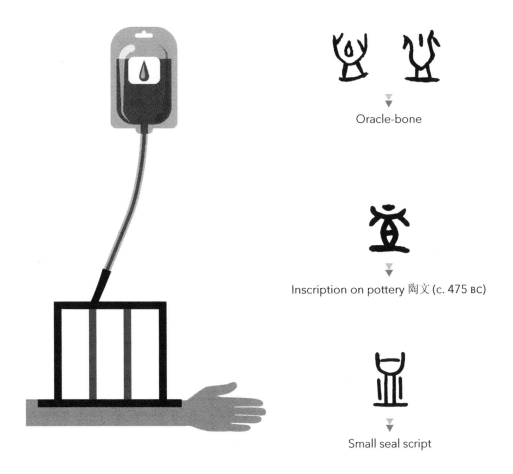

Oracle-bone

Inscription on pottery 陶文 (c. 475 BC)

Small seal script

- This character originally referred to the blood of the animals used for sacrificial offerings. It was later used to refer to human blood as well.
- Newly-made vessels require a blood sacrifice, known as 衈 [xìn] *vessels for animal blood sacrifice.*
- 嵇侍中血 [jī shì zhōng xuè] refers to *the blood of loyal officials*. The phrase came from the sacrificial death of Ji Kang's son, Ji Shao, who perished while protecting the emperor.

庆 to celebrate, to congratulate [qìng]

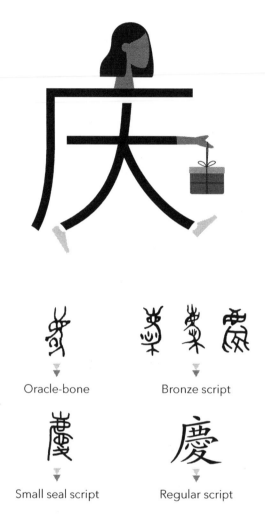

Oracle-bone

Bronze script

Small seal script

Regular script

- The compound ideograph in the oracle bone script for this character indicated the taking of a beautiful deer skin with sincerity to another household to celebrate.
- 弹冠相庆 [tán guān xiāng qìng] *to congratulate each other on promotions* is used negatively today. In ancient times, it was a positive phrase.
- During the Han Dynasty, 弹冠相庆 was used to describe sincere praise from friends, and denoted the beauty of friendship. Su Xun, a famous writer in the Northern Song Dynasty, began to use it in a negative way, describing relationships among evildoers. If an evil person was promoted, his accomplice or relatives would also gain advantages.

衣 apparel [yī]

Oracle-bone　　　　　Bronze script　　　　Small seal script

- This character is a pictograph. The top of the oracle bone script was the collar of a garment, and in the middle were the sleeves. At the bottom was the opening of the garment, which was fastened. The lapel opened to the left.
- In ancient times, people from the Central Plains favored the right-hand side. The lapels of their garments opened on the right, and were known as 右衽 [yòu rèn] *right lapel*. People outside of the Central Plains favored the left-hand side, regarded as 左衽 [zuǒ rèn] *left lapel*.
- The *upper outer garment* was called 衣, and the *bottom piece* was called 裳 [shang].
- Confucianism has strict rules regarding dressing etiquette.

守 to guard, to defend [shǒu]

Bronze script   Small seal script

- This is a compound ideographic character. The character's symbol in oracle bone script was a roof above a 寸 [cùn] *the point about one inch below the wrist*. This led to the idea of law. The ideograph 守 meant *to administer the law*.
- Another name for the house gecko was 守宫 [shǒu gōng]. It could be found on the walls of the palace, hunting for insects, metaphorically guarding the building.

汤 hot water, soup, boiling water, hot spring [tāng]

 → Bronze script

 → Small seal script

 → Regular script

- The original meaning of this character was *hot springs*. Japanese culture has upheld this true meaning.
- From its original meaning, it was extended to refer to hot boiling water. This was related to the ideograph of the blazing sun.
- The phrase 金汤 [jīn tāng] in the proverb 固若金汤 [gù ruò jīn tāng] *strong as iron, strongly fortified* is short for 金城汤池 [jīn chéng tāng chí] *a strong fortified city*. 金城 [jīn chéng] referred to a city made of gold – a strong, well-guarded city. 汤池 [tāng chí] denoted a moat filled with boiling water.
- The private land of the emperor, the empress, the princess, and other royal family members where tax was collected was also known as 汤沐邑 [tāng mù yì].

戏 to play, sport, game, drama [xì]

Bronze script

Small seal script

Regular script

- 戏 referred to the supporting role of the three armed military forces of ancient times.
- This character was considered as a compound ideograph representing the guard of honor of the armed forces. "Clothed in the attire of mythical animals, with military weapons in hands, showing off their prowess on the battlefield to build up the army's fighting spirit."
- Whether the character referred to the guard of honor or the supportive role in the three military forces, the initial idea was related to military matters.

异 extraordinary, unusual, different [yì]

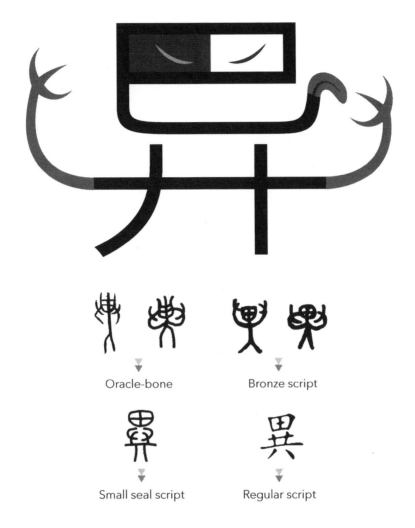

Oracle-bone

Bronze script

Small seal script

Regular script

- Shirakawa Shizuka, a Japanese scholar of Chinese literature, considered 异 to be a pictographic character. It resembles a ghoulish figure with two outspread arms, and is used to mean *strange, weird or different*.
- In Confucianism, lewd songs, outlandish clothing, uncanny feats, and strange wares were items and practices of mystery. Anybody found engaging in them would be executed.

尽 to exhaust, to the limit, to finish [jìn]

| Oracle-bone | Bronze script | Small seal script | Regular script |

- This is a compound ideograph. The pictographic character was a vessel with a hand holding a small brush, as if doing its best to clean it.
- Only when a vessel is completely empty can it be cleaned thoroughly. Therefore, the character's symbol in the oracle bone and metal scripts denoted *emptiness*.
- The character was also extended to mean *finished, the end*.

买 to buy [mǎi]

| Oracle-bone | Bronze script | Small seal script | Regular script |

- This is a compound ideograph. The character's symbol in oracle bone script was a net with a shell underneath, denoting the use of the net to catch shellfish.
- The character 卖 [mài] *to sell* has the symbol depicting *out* on top of 买. This expressed the idea that 卖 was to trade out a commodity.
- In ancient times, 质剂 [zhì jì] *a sales agreement* bound the buyer and the seller to the agreed terms and conditions of the sale. This was to avoid fraud.

束 to bind, to tie, to control [shù]

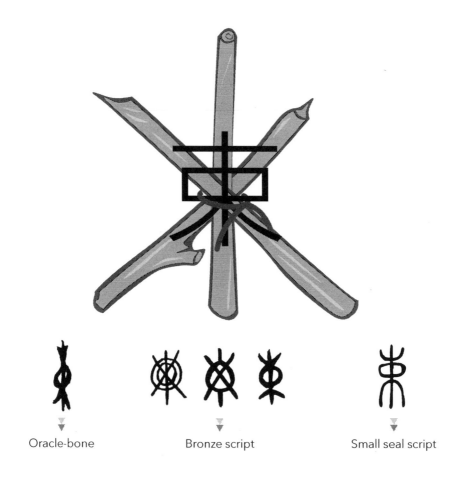

Oracle-bone   Bronze script   Small seal script

- This character was initially used as a quantifier. Ten of something constituted one 束.
- There was an unusual legal system in the Zhou Dynasty, known as 钧金束矢 [jūn jīn shù shǐ]. In this system, both parties involved in a lawsuit had to pay the same fee. The party who won the litigation would be reimbursed. The objective was to prove the difficulty of a litigation to the winning party, and indicate to the losing party that their loss outweighed the gains. This helped to resolve civil conflicts effectively.

丽 pretty, beautiful [lì]

| Oracle-bone | Bronze script | Small seal script | Regular script |

- This character did not originally refer to *beauty*. Its oracle bone script was a pictograph denoting a deer with two antlers.
- 丽 originally meant *to go or travel in a group,* or *to pair with.*
- 伉 [kàng] means *equal in force,* or *well matched.* 俪 [lì] refers to *a spouse, couple.* Therefore, 伉俪 is a well matched couple.
- 丽 was also used to mean a figure, a number.

豆　beans, legumes, an ancient cup or bowl with a stem [dòu]

Oracle-bone

Bronze script

Small seal script

- This character originally referred to a bowl with a long stem for holding meat. Therefore, in ancient texts the character resembled a tall stemmed plate.
- 豆 was used as a quantitative term; four units of 升 [shēng] *units of measurement* were equivalent to one 豆.
- Broomcorn millet, foxtail millet, sorghum, rice, hemp, beans (大豆 [dà dòu] *soy beans*), red beans, barley, and wheat were the nine grains that were the most important crops to cultivate in ancient times.

报 to report, to respond [bào]

Oracle-bone

Bronze script

Small seal script

Regular script

- This is a compound ideograph. The character's symbol in oracle bone script was a hand pinning down a kneeling person in a cangue. It denoted the idea of taking revenge.
- Both 当 [dāng] and 报 mean to *pass judgment on a case*.
- When used in different language environments, 报 can have two opposing meanings. It could mean 报复 [bào fù] *to take revenge*, and also 报恩 [bào ēn] *to repay gratitude*.
- 报 was also a type of sacrificial rite in ancient China. 烝报婚姻 [zhēng bào hūn yīn] referred to marriage or an extramarital affair with a woman of the older generation.

身 body, life [shēn]

Oracle-bone

Bronze script

Small seal script

- According to Xu Sheng's explanation in the *Shuowen Jiezi Dictionary*, 身 was a pictographic character. It resembled a human bowing in respect.
- After the Five Dynasties period, elderly women referred to themselves as 老身 [lǎo shēn] *an old woman*. This was an extension of the original idea of depicting a pregnant woman.
- The *Commentary of Zuo* used the phrase 二首六身 [èr shǒu liù shēn] to denote *longevity*.

狂 crazy, wild [kuáng]

Oracle-bone

Bronze script

Small seal script

- 狂 is a compound ideograph with phonetic complexities. The right-most part of its oracle bone script was the symbol for a fierce dog. In the bottom left was the character 王 [wáng] *king*, and above it was 止 [zhǐ] *leg*. This was the original character for 往 [wǎng] *to go, toward*. The character 狂 denoted a dog running out of control toward another place.
- The *Book of Han* recorded of the world's first case of rabies.
- The original idea of 狂 was a dog gone crazy, carrying negative connotations. It evolved through the years to mean *behaving without inhibitions or restraint*. Unrestrained behavior occurs when an ideal cannot become a reality – a cynical view of social norms.

龟 turtle, tortoise [guī]

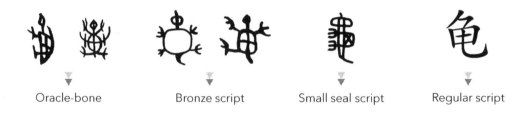

| Oracle-bone | Bronze script | Small seal script | Regular script |

- The oracle bone version of this character had six claws.
- The turtle was regarded as an auspicious animal due to its long lifespan. It was grouped together with the dragon, unicorn, and phoenix as the four divine beasts. The white turtle was more highly regarded than the rest.
- The phrase 龟藏六 [guī cáng liù] is an analogy used to refer to *a person hiding his wisdom, or living in seclusion, to avoid trouble arising from jealousy.* The short form 龟藏 [guī cáng] appeared often in ancient poetry.
- Using this character and its related forms as insults started during the Spring and Autumn Period. It was a requirement for a man who sold his wife or daughter to cover his head with a green towel to indicate his lowly status. That was how the phrase 绿帽子 [lǜ mào zi] *cuckold* (literally *green hat*) started. As the turtle's head is dark green, 龟 was therefore used to refer to a cuckold. A person who ran a brothel or acted as a pimp for his wife was also known as a 龟.

角 horn, bugle, role [jiǎo]

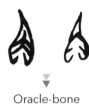

Oracle-bone

Bronze script

Small seal script

- The initial idea behind this character was the horn of a cow or goat. Later, it was extended to include the antlers of a deer and the horns of a rhinoceros. It was further extended to include all horn-shaped objects.
- People in ancient times used the term 总角之交 [zǒng jiǎo zhī jiāo] to mean *a friend from one's childhood*. 总角 [zǒng jiǎo] also means *a boy's hairstyle during his toddler years*.
- 角 can also be pronounced [jué]. This refers to a wine vessel in ancient times. There were strict rules for wine drinking in those days. Vessels had to match the status of the drinker.

饮 drink [yǐn]

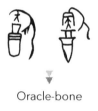

Oracle-bone

Bronze script

Small seal script

- In the Zhou Dynasty, there was an official post for a cup bearer. He was in charge of the *six types of drinks* called 六饮 [liù yǐn] for the emperor.
- The character 饮 referred to the action of keeping either water or wine in the mouth. It was extended to mean *to contain, to endure*, such as 饮恨 [yǐn hèn] *to nurse a grievance*.
- When used as a verb, the character is pronounced [yìn], denoting giving water to another person or a beast.

弟 younger brother [dì]

Oracle-bone

Bronze script

Small seal script

- This character was the original form of 第 [dì], an auxiliary word for ordinal numbers. There was an age order among brothers, which resulted in the character being extended to 弟弟 *little brother*.
- The younger brother was supposed to love and respect his older brother. This was referred to as 悌 [tì]. Therefore 弟 could be used interchangeably with 悌.
- 难兄难弟 [nàn xiong nàn dì] means that two brothers are exactly equal in terms of merits and virtues.

弃 to abandon, to discard [qì]

▽

Oracle-bone

▽

Bronze script

▽

Small seal script

▽

Regular script

– This is a compound ideograph. The character's oracle bone symbol was an infant with his head upright. Beside the character were three dots representing amniotic fluid. In the middle was a basket. Below it were two hands. The idea of the whole character was that a baby born in a posterior position had to be placed in a wicker basket and be disposed of. People in ancient times regarded unnatural births as bad luck, and babies born that way were discarded.

– The ancient penalty system included the tradition of 弃市 [qì shì] *public shaming of the criminal*, where people could spit at wrongdoers. The phrase was later used only for criminals sentenced to death.

– 弃其余鱼 [qì qí yú yú] meant *showing contentment through self-restraint and abstinence*.

君 monarch, sovereign [jūn]

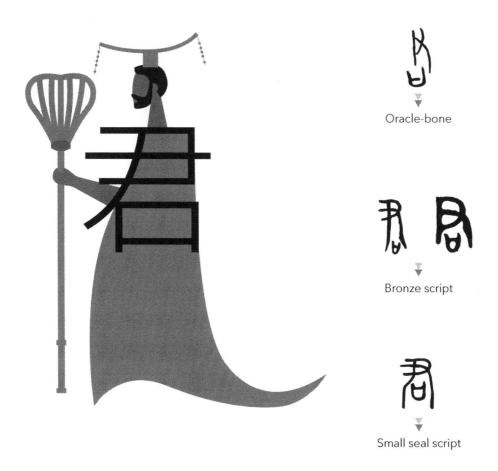

Oracle-bone

Bronze script

Small seal script

- This is an ideographic character denoting a chief sorcerer with a staff in his hand, chanting sacred text.
- The wife of Dong Fangshuo, a scholar in the Eastern Han Dynasty, was called 细君 [xì jūn], and this name was later used as a general term for *a wife*.
- Confucianism laid out detailed regulations and expectations for a 君子 [jūn zǐ] *a man of honor, a gentleman*.

鸡 chicken [jī]

Oracle-bone

Small seal script

Large seal script

Regular script

– The original version of this character was a pictograph. It later evolved into a compound ideograph, and was eventually transformed to a phono-semantic character. This transformation reflected the domestication process of a chicken.
– The chicken had the same status as a phoenix, and was used in sacrificial worship.
– People in ancient times regarded the 金鸡 [jīn jī] *golden rooster* as a symbol of amnesty.

雨　rain [yǔ / yù]

Oracle-bone

Bronze script

Small seal script

- This pictographic character was originally read in the fourth tone as a verb. Its symbol in oracle bone script was a horizontal line representing the sky, with six drops of rain coming down from it.
- The different types of rain in the twenty-four solar terms should be read in the fourth tone, as a verb.
- 旧雨新知 [jiù yǔ xīn zhī] refers to *old friends and new acquaintances*. The phrase came from a segment of the poet Du Fu's bitter life experience. He wrote of the melancholy of being ill and alone during autumn's rainy period. Old friends would visit regardless of the rain, but new acquaintances were deterred by the bad weather.

奔 to rush, to gallop [bēn]

Bronze script   Small seal script

- This compound ideographic character refers to running quickly. Its metal script was the image of a person swinging his arms. Below it were three legs, indicating the speed of his running.
- The *Rites of Zhou* contain details of a policy whereby unmarried people could attend a mass match-making session in order to waive the formalities of pre-marriage preparation. Consequently, 奔 was used to refer to a wedding that did not follow traditional rituals.
- 奔命 [bēn mìng] originally meant *to be on the run under the order of a higher authority*. This was extended to the phrase 疲于奔命 [pí yú bēn mìng] which meant *to be exhausted from running about on missions*. It later took on a negative connotation, referring to *being busy running about*. This phrase was initially written in the *Commentary of Zuo* as 罢于奔命 [bà yú bēn mìng].

取 to take, to get, to aim at [qǔ]

Oracle-bone

Bronze script

Small seal script

- This character originally meant *to capture*. The character's symbol in oracle bone script was an ear. The idea came from the ancient war-time practice of cutting off the enemy's left ear as evidence of a successful mission.
- 取 was the old form of the character 娶 [qǔ] *to marry a wife*. It was a common practice in ancient times to take a wife by force.
- Confucius was guilty of 以貌取人 [yǐ mào qǔ rén] *judging a person by his looks*. He admitted that he was taken in by Zai Wo's eloquence, and had been greatly disappointed by him. He also regretted the mistake he made in rejecting Zi Yu due to his unimpressive looks, for in doing so he lost a great disciple.

直 straight [zhí]

Oracle-bone

Bronze script

Small seal script

– The *Shuowen Jiezi Dictionary* explains this character as *uprightness*.
– Liu Xiahui was famed for his moral character. He insisted on upholding the principle of 直道
事人 [zhí dào shì rén] *a person on a straight path*.

虎 tiger [hǔ]

Oracle-bone

Bronze script

Small seal script

- This is a pictographic character. In oracle bone and metal scripts it resembled a tiger.
- The chamber pot was known as a 虎子 [hǔ zǐ] during the Han Dynasty because it was carved in the shape of a tiger. It was believed that General Li Guang shot dead a ferocious tiger, and ordered a chamber pot to be carved in its image to show his contempt for the beast. During the Tang Dynasty, the chamber pot was renamed 马子 [mǎ zi] to avoid disrespecting the name of Emperor Tang Gaozu's grandfather.
- 虎威 [hǔ wēi] *prowess of a general* was initially used to refer to the shape of a tiger bone.

齿 tooth [chǐ]

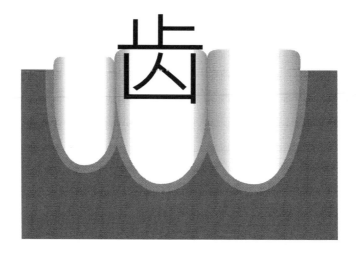

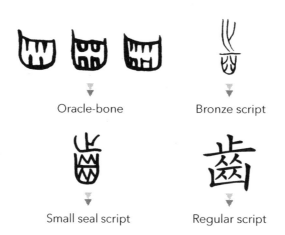

Oracle-bone   Bronze script

Small seal script   Regular script

- In ancient times, the front teeth were known as 齿 while the molars and premolars were known as 牙 [yá].
- As the number of teeth is related to a person's age, the character 齿 conferred the meaning of *age*. It was extended to objects with indentations that resembled teeth marks, and was subsequently used as a verb.
- There were records of tooth disease during the Yin Dynasty.
- The phrase 齿冷 [chǐ lěng] *to scorn* (literally *cold teeth*) carries the idea of the teeth being exposed to the cold as a person laughs scornfully at another.

兔 rabbit [tù]

Oracle-bone

Bronze script

Stone drums script
石鼓文 (475–221 BC)

Bronze script (逸)

Small seal script

- A rabbit seldom blinks. Its eyes are extraordinarily bright. Therefore 明视 [míng shì] - literally meaning *bright seeing* - was another name for the creature.
- 逸 [yì] *leisure, ease* is a compound ideograph. The character's symbol in metal script was a rabbit with the semantic 彳 [chì] on its left, to indicate *a road junction* or *to walk*. Below the character was 止 [zhǐ] to represent feet. It denoted the idea of the rabbit's ability to trick its opponent and run away.
- A person filing a lawsuit would feel helpless due to the injustice done to him, resembling a rabbit rushing around in search of an escape.

佩 to wear, to adorn [pèi]

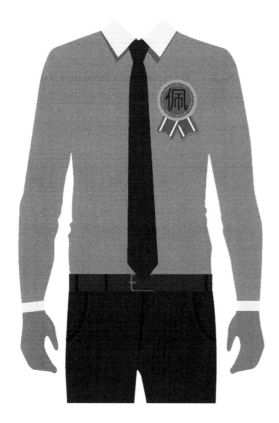

Bronze script

Small seal script

- The idea behind this character is *to attach a jade ornament to one's garment*.
- The attire of ancient government officials had to be tied with two types of belt. One was made of leather, and was worn under the outer garment. His 佩玉 [pèi yù] *jade*, official stamp, and coin pouch were attached to this belt.
- In ancient times, men of honor were expected to carry a jade ornament. Except when attending funerals, belts had to have jade ornaments attached to them. At funerals, all accessories, including these jade ornaments, were to be removed.

质 quality, nature, pawn [zhì]

Oracle-bone	Bronze script	Small seal script

- The original idea of this character was *collateral*. It meant using goods as a warrantee for money. Placing money as deposit in exchange for goods is called 贽 [zhuì].
- A trade agreement in ancient China was also known as 质; in the present day it is a 合同 [hé tong] *contract*.

京 a capital city [jīng]

Oracle-bone   Bronze script   Small seal script

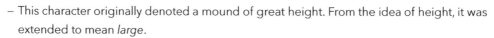

- This character originally denoted a mound of great height. From the idea of height, it was extended to mean *large*.
- The place where the emperor resided would doubtlessly be the largest city. Therefore, capital cities were known as 京师 [jīng shī], 京城 [jīng chéng], and 京都 [jīng dū].
- 京 was also used in numerals. One hundred million is one 兆 [zhào]. One billion is one 京. Ten billion is one 垓 [gāi].
- During wars in ancient times, the victors would pile the bodies of their enemies to a heap as proof of their conquest. These mass graves were known as 京观 [jīng guān].

实 real, reality, solid [shí]

Bronze script   Small seal script   Regular script

- This is a compound ideographic character, denoting money and food stored up for the family.
- 口实 [kǒu shí] refers to *excuse*. It used to *mean food in the mouth, regular discussions on the texts in oral reading,* and *an object contained in the mouth.*
- *The object contained in the mouth* differed from person to person, depending on his status. Liu Xiang remarked in the *Shuoyuan - Xiuwen,* "*Having an object in the mouth* is known as 唅 [hán]. The 唅实 [hán shí] *the object contained in the mouth* of the emperor is a pearl. In the mouths of the dukes and princes are jade, in the doctor's mouth is a keshi pearl, in the scholar's is a shell, and in the common people's, are grains."

学 to learn, to study, to mimic [xué]

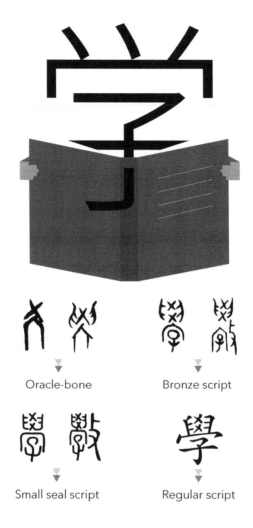

Oracle-bone

Bronze script

Small seal script

Regular script

— This character has evolved from the idea of a school building to the idea of learning. The process of change was reflected in the oracle bone and metal script.

— In ancient times, children began elementary school at the age of eight. When a pupil was fifteen, he would begin his university education. During the Western Zhou Dynasty, the university set up by the emperor was known as 辟雍 [pì yōng] *imperial university*. The university set up by the dukes and princes was called 宫 [gōng].

— The *ceremonial rite for the enrolment of a student* known as 释菜 [shì cài] has been lost over the generations. This was the offering of fruit and herbs in worship of the saint and scholar, Confucius. The ceremony included dancing and singing.

参 join [cān] / ginseng, the name of star [shēn]

Oracle-bone

Bronze script

Small seal script

参
Regular script

- This character is a compound ideograph. The oracle bone script was a person in profile. Above his head were three stars shining on him.
- 参星 [shēn xīng] *a star in the west* and 商星 [shāng xīng] *a star in the east* never meet. This referred to disharmony, or to mean that friends and relatives were separated and thus unable to meet.
- The three stars in the character are different sizes, denoting irregularity. 参差 [cēn cī] means *uneven, irregular.*

春 spring [chūn]

Oracle-bone

Bronze script

Small seal script

- Xu Shen, a scholar-official and philologist of the Eastern Han Dynasty, explained that when spring arrived, young shoots would begin to push their way out from the ground. Therefore, the character 推 [tuī] push is used to define this process.
- 春 is also another name for wine. A line in the classic poetry collection, *Shijing – Seventh Month*, reads "With this wine, I wish for a long life".
- 买春 [mǎi chūn] *to buy wine* was initially a very elegant phrase. It meant *to buy wine*, or *the act of enjoying the splendor of spring*.

相 each other, mutually [xiāng] / appearance [xiàng]

Oracle-bone

Bronze script

Small seal script

- This character has many different meanings. All of them were extended from 省视 [xǐng shì] *to examine carefully*, and 察看 [chá kàn] *to observe*.
- Because the eyes could see trees and other materials, anything that is connected is known as 相. When used to mean *mutual, or jointly*, the character is pronounced in its first tone – [xiāng].
- Another extension of the character's meaning is *to help*. It can also mean *the external appearance of a person*. The character is then pronounced in its fourth tone – [xiàng].
- 相公 [xiàng gong] originally referred to *the prime minister in ancient China*. As it was a formal address, the title was later used to refer to government officials. During the Qing Dynasty, it became another name for a male prostitute.

星 star [xīng]

Oracle-bone

Bronze script

Small seal script

- The Five Elements - Metal, Wood, Water, Fire and Earth – are called 星 *stars*. 辰 [chén] refers to the twenty-eight lunar mansions. The sun, moon, and stars made up 三辰 [sān chén].
- People in ancient times regarded the 恒星 [héng xīng] *stationary stars* as the essence of the world, set up in the sky.
- 恒星 were regarded as auspicious stars. 彗星 [huì xīng] comets are moving stars, and were considered unlucky.
- 小星 [xiǎo xīng] was another name for a concubine.

保 to protect, to keep, to defend [bǎo]

| Oracle-bone | Bronze script | Small seal script |

- This character's oracle bone script was an ideograph. On the left was a person with his back bending low. On the right was a child. The idea was carrying the child on one's back.
- The name 酒保 [jiǔ bǎo] *bartender* appeared very early in history. It is found twice in the book *He Guanzi* of the Warring States period.
- Yi Yin, the official who assisted the founding emperor of the Shang Dynasty build the state, was formerly a bartender.
- Both the terms 保庸 [bǎo yōng] and 庸保 [yōng bǎo] mean *the necessity of paying an employee the promised salary*. This way, the employee will be able to work in peace.

食 to eat, food [shí]

Oracle-bone

Bronze script

Small seal script

- In oracle bone script, this character was a pictograph. Below was a food container with a dot representing food. Above was a triangular cap.
- 六谷 [liù gǔ] *six grains* referred to paddy rice, broomcorn millet, millet, wheat, barley, and wild rice.
- People in ancient times had strict rules regarding 食. During the pre-Qin period, they ate two meals a day. The Qin Emperor later changed it to three.
- The character could also mean abandon, as in the phrase 食言 [shí yán] *to go back on one's word*.
- 三食 [sān shí] not only referred to three meals a day, but also to an unworthy son selling the family's land, books, and slaves for his own survival.

侯 marquis [hóu]

Oracle-bone   Bronze script   Small seal script

— This pictographic character has a piece of leather or cloth at the top and right side to represent a target. Below it is an arrow, which has hit the target.
— 射侯 [shè hóu] *archery target* denoted using an arrow to hit a target. If the target was made of leather, it was called a 皮侯 [pí hóu], and if it was made of fabric, it was called a 布侯 [bù hóu].
— After an archery session, the players who had hit targets had to offer cups of wine. This led to those who received land allocations from the emperor being known as 诸侯 [zhū hóu].
— Ancient scholars often considered the character 侯 in 侯禳 [hóu ráng] *ceremonial rites to ward off evil*, and 候 [hòu] *await* as interchangeable. Some said that after a period of time, evil (corruption) would be averted.

亲 relative, parents [qīn]

Oracle-bone

Bronze script

Small seal script

Regular script

- In ancient times, there was a phrase 六亲 [liù qīn] *the six family relations*. There were different explanations for it. One was that the six relations were the father, son, older brother, younger brother, husband, and wife. Another held that it referred to the father, mother, older brother, younger brother, wife, and son. Yet another explanation was that the phrase meant father-son, brothers, sisters of the father, maternal uncle and his sons, marriage, and relations by marriage.

- When two families are united by marriage, the in-laws are called 亲家 [qìng jia]. Using the fourth tone in this phrase had its origins in the Eastern Han Dynasty.

首 head, leader, chief [shǒu]

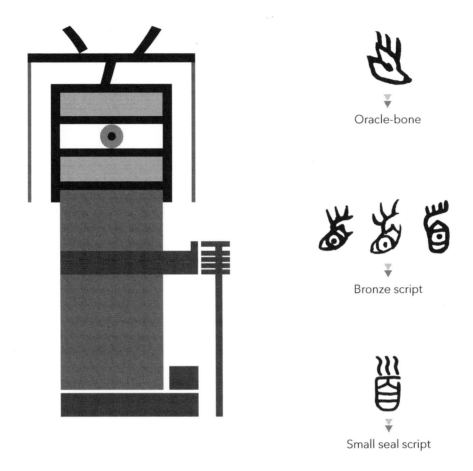

Oracle-bone

Bronze script

Small seal script

- The term 首级 [shǒu jí] *a decapitated head* had its origins in the Shang Yang Reforms. A military awarding system was set up during battles; each decapitated head led to a promotion of one grade. Later, the phrase became the system's name.
- Ancient monarchs and modern-day leaders are known as 元首 [yuán shǒu]. The character 元 also denotes *head*. This title was already being used during the Zhou Dynasty.
- Yearning for one's hometown, or returning a body for burial in its hometown, were both expressed as 首丘 [shǒu qiū].
- 面首 [miàn shǒu] *a catamite* was used more positively in earlier times, to mean a very good looking man.

壼 kettle, pot, flask [hú]

Oracle-bone

Bronze script

Small seal script

Regular script

- During a feast, the minister, the senior official, and the scholar would use a quadrangle pot to match their status and rank. It also signified the uprightness of their offices. Soldiers would use a round pot, denoting submission to orders.
- 方丈 [fāng zhàng] refers to a Buddhist abbot. The term was borrowed from a Taoist title when Buddhism entered China.
- One of the games played during a feast was 投壺 [tóu hú]. The host and guests took turns to throw arrows into a pot. The one who threw in the most arrows was the winner. The penalty for losing was to drink. People in ancient times considered this game to be the quaintest of all.

获 to capture, to obtain [huò]

Oracle-bone

Bronze script

Small seal script

Regular script

- This is a compound ideographic character. The earliest ancient version was 隻 [zhī] *the complex character for a single unit*, with 隹 [zhuī] *a bird with a short tail* at the top, and a hand below, denoting the capturing of a bird with a hand.
- Hunted animals were known as 獲 [huò], and harvested crops were known as 穫 [huò]. Both were simplified into 获.
- From the idea of hunted animals, the character was extended to denote a female slave.

班 class, team, shift [bān]

班 班 班
Bronze script

班
Small seal script

- This character originally meant *to divide jade equally*. It was extended to mean *separate*, or *leaving the team*. Therefore 班马 [bān mǎ] *zebra* denotes a horse that has left the team.
- From the idea of dividing the jade of a feudal lord, the character was extended to mean *return*, like the return of the army that had been sent out.
- After the jade was divided, the pieces had to be arranged in a specified order. This led to the extension of the character to mean *order, job levels*. It also means *a unit of a bigger body*. One example is 班子 [bān zi] *an organization set up for a mission*.

射 to shoot, to fire [shè]

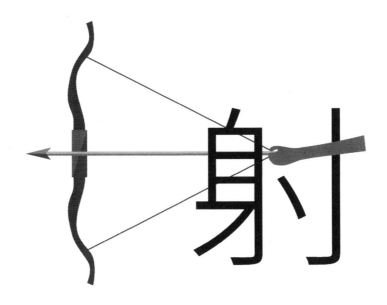

| Oracle-bone | Bronze script | Small seal script |

- This is a compound ideograph. The oracle bone script was the image of a bow and arrow, denoting pulling the string of a bow to shoot the arrow.
- The character's original idea was shooting an arrow.
- In past times, local archery ceremonies involved music. Participants were required to shoot to the rhythm of the music and aim at the bull's eye.
- There were five kinds of archery in these ancient ceremonies.

徒 apprentice, pupil [tú]

| Oracle-bone | Bronze script | Small seal script |

- The original idea of this character was 徒步行走 [tú bù xíng zǒu] *hiking*. In ancient times, 徒步 referred to common people.
- Soldiers in ancient times were also known as 徒步. The infantry comprised of many soldiers, therefore 徒 was extended to mean *many people*. Since the infantry is one unit in the army, the meaning of 徒 has extended to denote *the same type*, or *the same category of people*, like 徒党 [tú dǎng] *followers*, 门徒 [mén tú] *disciples*, and 徒弟 [tú di] *apprentice*.
- The original idea of 徒 is walking without the help of a vehicle. This led to the idea of 出空 [chū kōng] *being empty*, and 徒手 [tú shǒu] *bare-handed*.

乘 to ride, to take advantage of [chéng] / a war chariot drawn by four horses [shèng]

Oracle-bone

Bronze script

Small seal script

- The oracle bone script for this character clearly depicted the original idea of *ascending, rising*, as in a person ascending a tree.
- As a horse runs, it picks up speed. This brought an extension of the meaning to 乘势 [chéng shì] *to strike while the iron is hot*. Riding a horse makes use of the creature's speed, leading to another extension of meaning to *making use of, relying on, taking advantage of*. When used this way, the character is pronounced [chéng].
- 万乘 [wàn shèng] referred to ten thousand carriages, which denoted the emperor. 千乘 [qiān shèng] referred to one thousand carriages, i.e. the vassal system. 百乘 [bǎi shèng] referred to one hundred carriages, meaning the system of the feudal officials.

sacrificial wine, bow case [chàng]

| Oracle-bone | Bronze script | Small seal script |

— This is a pictographic character resembling a vessel for holding things. The container was on top, and below it was its stem.

— Monarchs in ancient times built altars out of green, amber, white, black, and yellow earth. Green represented the east, red represented the south, white represented the west, and black represented the north. The top was covered with yellow earth. When allocating land to the marquis and dukes, one color of earth was collected from every piece of land, then covered with yellow earth and wrapped with cogon grass before being presented to the marquis and dukes.

— *The Records of Wangdu* state that "The emperor holds sacrificial wine, the marquis holds lavender, the senior official holds orchids, the scholar holds mugwort, and the common people hold wormwood."

造 to make, to build [zào]

Bronze script

Small seal script

- This character was originally written as 艁. Its compound ideograph points to sacrificial offerings in a 舟 [zhōu] *boat*.
- The six practices of worshipping spiritual beings to avert misfortune were called 六祈 [liù qí].
- When the phrase 造舟 [zào zhōu] *to build a boat* was used to mean *a gift to the emperor*, it denoted the wedding ceremony of a monarch.

旅 brigade, troops, to travel [lǚ]

Oracle-bone

Bronze script

Small seal script

- The original idea of this character was the organization of an army. Five hundred soldiers made one 旅 *brigade*. From the idea of the army moving out, it was extended to mean *travelling*, which is more frequently used nowadays.
- 逆旅 [nì lǚ] denotes receiving guests at a hotel. Therefore, the phrase is used to refer to an *inn*, or *hotel*.
- Wild vegetation that is not grown by sowing seeds is called 旅.

疾 disease, sickness [jí]

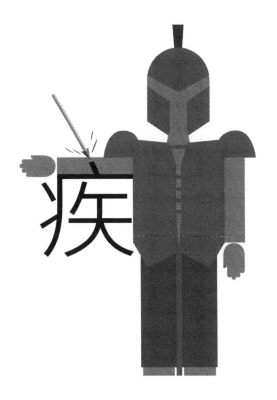

Oracle-bone

Bronze script

Ancient Text

Small seal script

- This is a compound ideograph. The character's symbol on the left of the oracle bone script was a person standing erect, having been hit by an arrow below his right armpit.
- 疾 is a mild sickness. When accumulated, it becomes 病 [bìng] *illness*, which is more serious than 疾.
- Buddhists called illnesess 维摩疾 [wéi mó jí]. Common scholars and officials called them 狗马疾 [gǒu mǎ jí].

桑 mulberry [sāng]

Oracle-bone

Eave tile script of Western Han
西汉瓦当 (c. 200 BC)

Small seal script

- The oracle bone script for this character was a pictograph of a mulberry tree.
- 桑梓 [sāng zǐ] meant *homeland*, where trees were planted by parents. Therefore, people in ancient times used the phrase to mean both *homeland* and *elders*.
- 桑间濮上 [sāng jiān pú shàng] *rendezvous for lovers* was originally the name of a specific place. Later it evolved to become the name of any place where lovers meet. It also came to denote a locale notorious for profligacy.

黄 yellow [huáng]

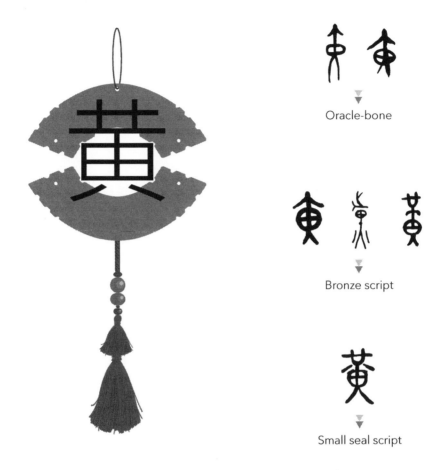

Oracle-bone

Bronze script

Small seal script

- The *Shuowen Jiezi Dictionary* states that yellow is "the color of the ground." This is an extension of the meaning of the character. Its original meaning was 佩璜 [pèi huáng] *jade*.
- According to experts on the Five Elements, yellow is one of the five pure colors along with bluish green, amber, white, and black. As it was in the middle, it was regarded highly by people in ancient times, and became the color of royalty.

得 to get, to obtain [dé]

Oracle-bone   Bronze script   Small seal script

- This character's symbol in the oracle bone script denoted the idea of having gone through the long and slow process of obtaining a cowrie. The cowrie was very precious because it was hard to obtain, therefore the character also denoted satisfaction.
- The phrase 得鱼忘筌 [dé yú wàng quán] *to forget the means by which the end is attained* appeared in *Zhuangzi*. It was used to describe a person who succeeds in a task then forgets the help that got him there.

庶 numerous [shù]

Oracle-bone

Bronze script

Small seal script

- The original idea of this character was heating up a stone (pot) with fire to cook. The character was formed by combining pictographic symbols of practical daily life in ancient times with phonetic value. The pot could contain different types of food; this led to the idea of *numerous*, and *a variety of*.

- 庶出 [shù chū] *the offspring of a concubine* has its origins in the eating etiquette of ancient times. Besides the main course, there was an appetizing hors d'oeuvres that was considered as a side dish. This was known as 庶羞 [shù xiū] *a variety of delicacies*. The phrase was later used to refer to a child born of a wife other than the first.

敝 broken [bì]

Oracle-bone

Stone script of Qin
(The Curse of Chu)
秦代石刻《诅楚文》

Small seal script

- This is a compound ideogram. The character's symbol in oracle bone script had a scarf on the left. On the right was a hand holding a stick, tearing the scarf.
- 敝膝 [bì xī] was a knee-length adornment attached to the front of a garment. It was usually made of leather, and its function was to conceal. It was not an apron. 犊鼻 [dú bí] when pronounced in its short form [kūn] referred to *an apron*.
- The phrase 敝帷不弃 [bǐ wéi bù qì] had many explanations, but the most common was *old items that still have use*. The original meaning of *burying a horse* was either ignored or covered up.

渔 fishing [yú]

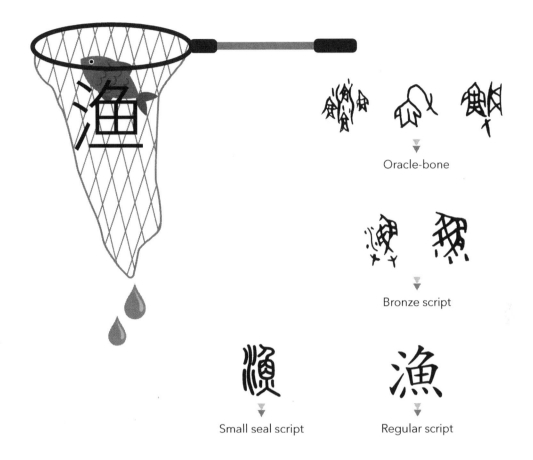

Oracle-bone

Bronze script

Small seal script

Regular script

- In ancient times, there was an official position for a 渔师 [yú shī] who was responsible for fishing, providing fish for worship offerings and feasts.
- 渔猎 [yú liè] was used to mean *philandering*. 下渔色 [xià yú sè] referred to marrying a wife and a concubine in one's own country.
- 猎艳 [liè yàn] *to philander with women* originally referred to a quest for splendor, but eventually took on the same connotation as 渔色 [yú sè] *to seek carnal pleasure*.

黑 black [hēi]

Oracle-bone   Bronze script   Small seal script

- The *Shuowen Jiezi Dictionary* states that, according to the lesser seal script, black was the color that resulted from smoke. There was fire below, and the chimney above it was blackened by smoke, denoting the color black.
- According to experts on the Five Elements, the east was green; the south was red; the west was white; the north was black, and the earth was yellow. The north was also water, represented by the color black.
- Black used to be the royal color, denoting the emperor. It was later changed to yellow. The flourishing of Buddhism could be the reason for the demotion of the color's status. Buddhist teachings rendered evil as 黑业 [hēi yè] *evil deeds*. "The people who practiced evil did not do good. As a result, they would receive their retribution after death. Their spirits would suffer in hell. Their suffering would be great. Therefore it was defined as 黑 black."
- In ancient times, 黑头 [hēi tóu] referred to *youths*, and 黑子 [hēi zǐ] meant *mole*.

遗 to offer as a gift [wèi] / to lose, to omit [yí]

Bronze script

Small seal script

Regular script

— The oracle bone script for this character was a compound ideograph, carrying the idea of presenting a shell to someone with two hands.

— Looking from the giver's point, once the gift was given, it was the same as having lost it. Therefore 遗 was extended to mean *to lose, to abandon, to be left over, to forget*. When used this way, the character is read as [yí].

— 遗簪 [yí zān] is used to mean *old items* or *old relationships*.

集 to gather, to assemble, to collect [jí]

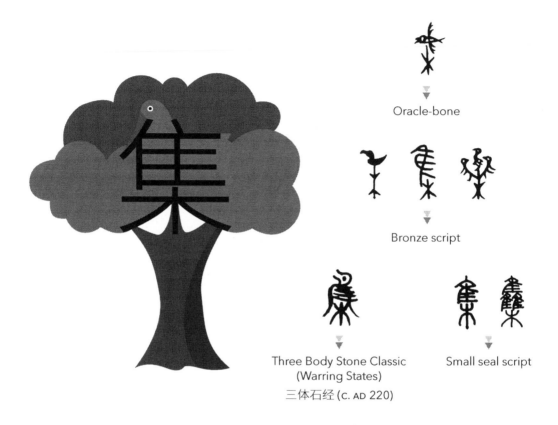

Oracle-bone

Bronze script

Three Body Stone Classic
(Warring States)
三体石经 (c. AD 220)

Small seal script

- This character is a compound ideogram. Its character symbol in metal script was an image of three birds on the tree.
- Birds will gather on the trees in flocks when they complete a part of their journey. 集 was therefore extended to mean *accomplishment*, or *success*.
- From the gathering of a flock of birds, the character was again extended to mean *to stay for a time, to assemble,* or *to stabilize.* It can also be used as a noun, like 诗集 [shī jí] *a poetry collection*.

御 Imperial, of an emperor [yù]

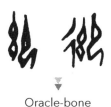

Oracle-bone

Bronze script

Small seal script

- The original idea of this character was driving a horse carriage. It was extended to denote controlling everything (vehicles) that moved on land or flew in the air.
- From the idea of controlling the reins, it was extended to denote ruling and governing. The highest ruler was the emperor. Consequently, everything that the emperor did and everything he used had the term 御 attached to it. The forbidden area in the palace was also known as 御.
- In the imperial harem were the Empress, the three Madames, nine imperial concubines, twenty-seven hereditary consorts, and eighty-one imperial wives. The eighty-one wives were managed by the hereditary consorts. Eighty-one is the square of nine, therefore they were also known as 九御 [jiǔ yù] or 女御 [nǔ yù]. They were the ones who took care of the emperor's sleep.

童 child [tóng]

Bronze script

Small seal script

- The original idea of this character was a male slave.
- Male slaves and children were not required to wear their hair in a bun, so the character was extended to mean *children who have not reached puberty*, calling them 童子 [tóng zǐ] *a boy child*, or 儿童 [ér tóng] *children*. 童蒙 [tóng méng] meant *childish ignorance*.
- 小童 [xiǎo tóng] was the name by which the wife of a monarch would address herself.

寒 cold, afraid [hán]

Bronze script

Small seal script

- This character was originally rather complex. Its metal script version had a house at the top. In the house were many things. In the middle was a person with his foot bent under him. The two horizontal lines at the bottom represented ice. Around it were four bunches of grass to stave off the cold.
- Three signs augur the arrival of the period of Cold Dew in the traditional calendar. The first is the appearance of the swan goose. The second is the sparrow entering the water for clams. The third is the blooming of the yellow chrysanthemum.
- The three signs of 小寒 [xiǎo hán] *the period of the Slight Cold (23ʳᵈ solar term)* are the wild geese flying north, the magpie building its nest, and the pheasants beginning to call.
- 大寒 [dà hán] *the period of the Great Cold (24ᵗʰ solar term)* has three features. Chickens will hatch chicks, birds of prey will fly in the sky hunting for their prey, and the middle of the rivers or lakes will be frozen hard.

雇 to hire, to employ [gù]

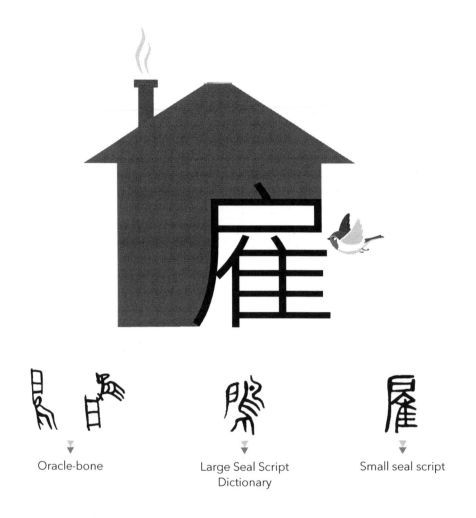

Oracle-bone

Large Seal Script
Dictionary

Small seal script

- This character was read as [hù] in earlier times. It referred to a kind of migrating bird that was related to farming and sericulture. It was used to remind farmers not to be lazy and miss the farming season. From this idea, it led to the notion of *to borrow, to take advantage of*, and was extended to mean *to hire*.
- There were nine types of birds for the purpose of 雇, each used for different functions.

寓 residence [yù]

Bronze script

Houma Covenant
(Spring and Autumn
Period) 侯马盟书
(c. 1400 BC)

Small seal script

- The original idea of 禺 [yú] was related to macaques. In 寓, a house has been added to the original character, meaning *to provide people with a temporary place to seek pleasure*. This led to the extension of the idea of *living away from home*, or *entrusting oneself to the care of somebody*. It also carries the notion of *looking on*.
- 寓公 [yù gōng] referred to noblemen who had lost their land and had to live in other countries. It was extended to refer to former government officials and gentry in exile.
- People in ancient times believed that ghosts had heads as big as buckets, and could pin a person down on his bed.

奠 to establish, to settle, to make offerings to the spirits of the dead [diàn]

Oracle-bone

Bronze script　　　　　　　　　　Small seal script

- This character originally referred to making offerings of wine and food to the spirits of the dead.
- In ancient times, when a daughter was getting married, the family would use fish and 苹藻 [píng zǎo] *a name for an offering* in ancestor worship; this type of offering was known as 濡苹实俎 [rú píng shí zǔ]. The groom had to go to the bride's house to escort her back to his residence. He also had to present a wild goose as a gift. This practice was called 奠雁迎门 [diàn yàn yíng mén].
- The idea of 奠 was to set wine and food as an offering. Therefore, the wine jars had to be placed in a stable position either on the floor or the altar. This led to the extension of the character to mean *being stable*, as in the phrase 奠基 [diàn jī] *to lay a foundation*.

登 to ascend, to mount, to publish [dēng]

Oracle-bone

Bronze script

Small seal script

- This is a compound ideographic character, denoting two hands holding a vessel full of beans as an offering, and ascending the steps to the ancestral temple.
- According to the classic Chinese text encyclopedia *Lüshi Chunqiu*, the midsummer month, which was the fifth month in the lunar calendar, was 农乃登黍 [nóng nǎi dēng shǔ]. This referred to the harvest rite in which farmers had to make offerings of the first harvest of broomcorn millet. Consequently, 登 was used to denote *ripe*, or *bountiful harvest*.
- 登 also refers to squat, as in 登坑 [dēng kēng] *to be higher than the latrine*, or *to squat above the latrine*.

鼓 drum, drum-like things [gǔ]

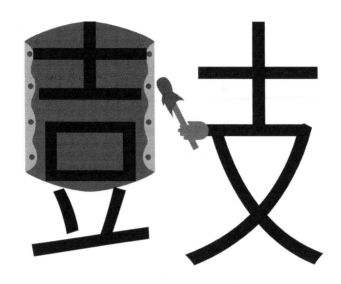

| Oracle-bone | Bronze script | Small seal script |

- This is a compound ideographic character. On the left in the oracle bone version was an image of a drum. On the left was a hand. In the middle was a drum stick about to hit the drum.
- According to the *Rites of Zhou*, there was an official position for a drummer. His role was to master and teach the six types of drums and the four types of metal instruments.
- The character was originally a noun. It was later used as a verb, which brought in different meanings, such as 击鼓进攻 [jī gǔ jìn gōng] *drumming for attack*, 敲击弹奏 [qiāo jī tán zòu] *making music with percussion instruments*, 摇动 [yáo dòng] *to shake or sway*, 鼓动 [gǔ dòng] *to instigate*, and many more. A fun way of using it is in 鼓腹 [gǔ fù] *eating all day and not doing anything else*. Another example is in 鼓舌 [gǔ shé] *using artful talk to show off one's glibness in speech or wit*.

献 to offer, to present, to show [xiàn]

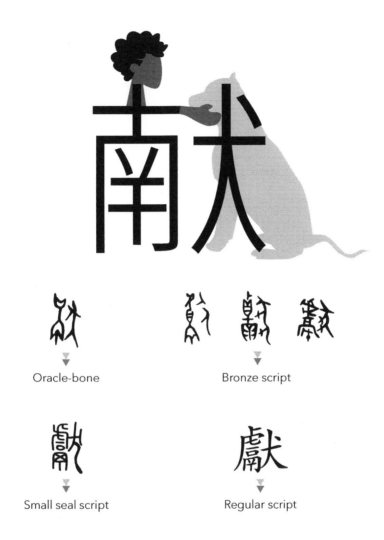

Oracle-bone

Bronze script

Small seal script

Regular script

- 羹献 [gēng xiàn] was a sacrificial offering of dogs to the spiritual beings after the dogs had been fed and fattened with leftover food. The character 献 denotes an offering.
- During ancestral worship in ancient times, there was a rite known as 三献 [sān xiàn], in which wine was offered three times.
- 三献玉 [sān xiàn yù] referred to the idea that it was very difficult to for a person with talents to make a bosom friend. This idea originated from the story 和氏璧 [hé shì bì].
- 献曝 [xiàn pù] and 献芹 [xiàn qín] both mean *self-deprecating of one's gifts*, or *suggestions*.

虞 to worry, to predict [yú]

Bronze script

Small seal script

- The original idea of this character was *to dance and sing in a tiger's skin*.
- 驺虞 [zōu yú] *a fabled animal like a black spotted tiger* was a kindhearted and righteous beast. It only ate dead animals, would not harm other creatures, had the virtue of sparing animals' lives.
- Sacrifices were offered to the spirits to prevent them from doing any harm. This idea brought out the idea of anxiety and suffering, as shown in the phrase 四方无虞 [sì fāng wú yú] *no worries in any direction*. If there was a risk of suffering, preventive measures had to be taken. This again led to the idea of prevention, or *to expect beforehand*. 不虞 [bù yú] means *unexpected*.

寢 to sleep [qǐn]

| Oracle-bone | Bronze script | Small seal script |

- The character 寢 [qǐn] referred to sleeping in a normal situation. However, when the character 寝 [qǐn] was used, it referred to lying down when ill. Eventually there was no differentiation between the two, and the common character to use was 寢.
- The *Book of Rites* contained a regulation that 寢 should involve lying down on the bed, not napping at the table.
- 寢 can be used in a very interesting way, as an adjective to mean *ugly*.

疑 to suspect, to doubt [yi]

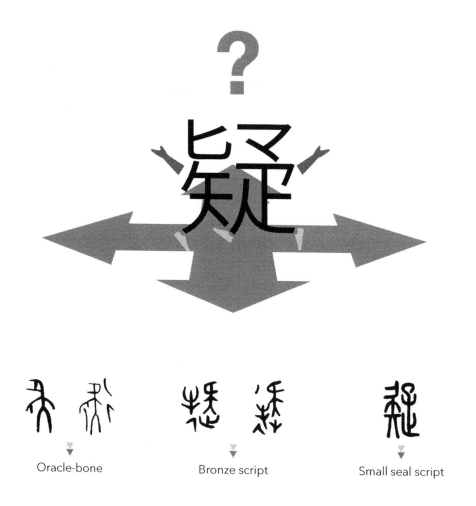

| Oracle-bone | Bronze script | Small seal script |

- The original idea of this character was *feeling lost and uncertain at a crossroad*.
- 犹 [yóu] or 犹猢 [yóu hú] was a kind of primate with a very suspicious nature. Every time the grass moved with the wind, it scampered up a tree to observe the situation. When it was sure that there was no danger, it would come down again, looking around nervously, ready to scamper back up at any sign of peril. This way of mentally torturing of oneself gave rise to the phrase 犹疑 [yóu yi] hesitation.
- According to legend, the emperor had four ministers who assisted him in the governing of the country. The role of 疑 was to answer to the emperor's questions. The role of 丞 [chéng] *assistant officer* was to keep records. The role of 辅 [fǔ] *to assist* was to correct wrongs. The role of 弼 [bì] *to assist* was to spread news. Together, the four were known as 疑丞 and 辅弼.

彝 wine vessel [yí]

Oracle-bone   Bronze script   Small seal script

— The idea of this character was using two hands to present a bird or chicken as a sacrificial offering to the divine beings or ancestors.

— During the Zhou Dynasty, there was an official position for a 司尊彝 [zūn yí] *the official responsible for the six wine vessels for sacrificial offerings during ritual ceremonies.*

BIO OF XU HUI

Born in 1969, Xu Hui is a freelance writer, presently residing in Dali, Yunnan. He was the chief editor for *Temperament of the Sixties, The Backdoor of Chinese History,* and other works, and co-author of *The New Shuowen Interpretation, The Chinese Language Dictionary,* and the series *Looking at History the Fun Way*. His books include *The Art of Body Charm: Body Politics in Chinese History, Troubled Times Specimens: Personality Disorder in Chinese History, The Whip of Troubled Times: Thirty Most Controversial People in Chinese History, The Most Misunderstood Idioms of the Chinese People,* and *Enlightening Interpretation of Chinese Phrases.*

BIO OF JULIE LOO

Julie Loo, a former principal of Shanghai Singapore International School, XuHui Campus, has been in the education field in Singapore and Shanghai for more than 28 years. Being an educator, she shares the author's passion in wanting people learning Chinese Language to appreciate the beauty of the language.